Roman Amphitheaters

Roman Amphitheaters

Don Nardo

Watts LIBRARY

Franklin Watts
A Division of Scholastic Inc.
New York • Toronto • London • Auckland • Sydney
Mexico City • New Delhi • Hong Kong
Danbury, Connecticut

Note to readers: Definitions for words in **bold** can be found in the Glossary at the back of this book.

Photographs ©: AP/Wide World Photos/Bruno Mosconi: 47; Archive Photos: 12; Art Resource, NY/Erich Lessing: 24; Christie's Images: 36; Corbis-Bettmann: 14 (John Heseltine), 45 (Archivo Iconografico, S.A,), 5 bottom, 42 (Mimmo Jodice), 2 (Charles F. Rotkin), 32 (Roger Wood); H. Armstrong Roberts/George Hunter, Inc.: 5 top, 40; Mary Evans Picture Library: 28, 31, 43; National Geographic Image Collection: 20 (H.M. Herget); Photri: 8, 26 (Index), 29 (Shelly Smith), 21 bottom; Stock Montage, Inc.: 19, 37; Superstock, Inc.: 35 (A.K.G. Berlin), cover; The Art Archive: 10 (Harper Collins Publishers), 17 (J. Enrique Molina/Album), 9, 21 top, 38 (Dagli Orti); The Image Works: 6 (Bill Bachmann), 16 (1. Greenberg), 22 (Brian Yarvin).

The photograph on the cover and the photograph opposite the title page show the Colosseum in Rome, Italy.

Library of Congress Cataloging-in-Publication Data

Nardo, Don, 1947-
     Roman amphitheaters / Don Nardo.
         p. cm.—(Watts library)
     Includes bibliographical references and index.
     ISBN 0-531-12036-8 (lib. bdg.)   0-531-16224-9 (pbk.)
     1. Amphitheaters—Rome—Juvenile literature. 2. Architecture, Roman—Juvenile literature.
3. Colosseum (Rome, Italy)—Juvenile literature. [1. Amphitheaters. 2. Architecture—Rome.
3. Rome—Antiquities.] I. Title II. Series
NA313.N37 2002
725'.827'0937—dc21

                                                                                           2001017769

Contents

The Colosseum is still as much of a marvel today as it was in ancient times.

Chapter One

Rome's Early Wooden Arenas

Almost every modern traveler to Rome, the capital city of Italy, eventually finds his or her way to a street called the Piazzale de Colosseo. There, the ruins of a huge ancient structure—the famous Colosseum—dominate the scene. It is shaped like a gigantic oval bowl. And it is enclosed by a tall, curving stone wall, much of it still intact after the passage of

7

A "Double Theater"

The term *amphitheater* comes from Latin, the language of the ancient Romans. The original word is *amphitheatrum* meaning "double theater." A typical Roman theater was shaped like a **hemisphere** or a half-circle. And an amphitheater looked like two hemispheres joined together to form an oval.

almost two thousand years. What makes that wall so distinctive is that it is made up of three rows of elegant arches stacked on top of one another. Overall, the structure towers more than 150 feet (46 meters) into the sky, and it is hundreds of feet wide, dwarfing the cars and people on the nearby street.

In the great open space inside the Colosseum's bowl, all is quiet, save for the chatter of a few tourists and the occasional chirping of birds. But long ago, when the building was new, huge crowds gathered in this space. They came to see men, women, and animals fight to the death. These exciting but brutal contests were part of the renowned public games of the ancient Romans. The Romans built many structures like the Colosseum, which they called **amphitheaters**. Such buildings were also referred to more informally as **arenas**—the name of the central areas on the floor of the amphitheaters, where the actual fighting took place.

As the civilization of Rome developed, the Romans created a very powerful army.

Military Skill and Sheer Determination

The remains of the Colosseum and other amphitheaters make up only a small portion of the Roman ruins that dot the landscapes of Europe, North Africa, and the Near East. These ruins are evidence that the ancient Romans conquered many lands and peoples. Indeed, through military skill and sheer determination, they built one of the largest and most influential empires in world history. Even after Rome declined and fell, its language and many of its ideas and customs went on to shape later societies in important ways.

Rome began as a small, modest farming community, with primitive huts made of **thatch**, bundled plant stems

9

The Roman Army

The Roman army became the most effective military organization in the ancient world. It consisted of many **legions**, each a group of about five thousand men that traveled, camped, and fought together. The soldiers, called legionaries, were tough, highly trained, and equipped with swords, shields, and spears.

This photograph shows a statue of Augustus, the first emperor of Rome.

and branches. These huts first appeared on seven low hills near the Tiber River, in western Italy, about three thousand years ago. Over time, the inhabitants became highly organized and developed a strong army.

With that army, Rome slowly expanded its empire. First it conquered its immediate neighbors, and later it took control of all Italy. Then the Romans built a navy and extended their rule over other peoples living along the shores of the Mediterranean Sea. By the first century B.C., about two thousand years ago, the Roman realm stretched from Spain in the west to Palestine (now the nation of Israel) in the east.

Through most of these years, the Roman government was a republic, controlled largely by a legislature known as the Senate. In the late first century B.C., however, a series of terrible civil wars caused the Roman Republic to fall. And in its place, a strong ruler named Augustus created the Roman Empire. This was a government and a realm controlled mainly by a single man—the emperor, who had enormous powers.

The World's Greatest Builders

It was in the early years of the Empire that the Colosseum and most of the other large amphitheaters were erected. These structures show clearly that the Romans were not merely soldiers and conquerors. They were also great builders. In fact, they were without doubt the most skilled and successful builders in the whole ancient world. In addition to their amphitheaters, which could seat tens of thousands of people, they erected hundreds of bridges, enormous bathhouses, theaters, racetracks, and stone temples. They also constructed thousands of miles of paved roads and water channels called **aqueducts**.

Because the Romans were a very practical people, they created these structures to fulfill specific needs. The aqueducts, for example, brought millions of gallons a day of life-giving water to Roman cities. And the roads and bridges made it easier for soldiers and traders to reach various parts of the realm.

11

The Need for Amphitheaters

The Romans also perceived a need for structures to house their public games. For chariot racing, one of their favorite pastimes, they early built a long racetrack, or **circus**, known as the Circus Maximus or "Great Circus." At first, it was no more than a open field with some wooden bleachers set up along the sides. But over time stone seats replaced the wooden ones. And large statues and other decorations were added. These and other changes made the building very elaborate and impressive.

For a long time, however, the Romans had no buildings designed specifically to present fights among animals and trained public fighters known as **gladiators**. Instead, they staged these fights in open areas, most commonly a city's main square, or **forum**. We know that the Romans originally staged

An Amphitheater Collapses

The worst known case of an ancient wooden amphitheater collapsing occurred in A.D. 27 at Fidenae, a town not far north of Rome. According to the first-century A.D. Roman historian Tacitus: "An ex-slave named Atilius started building an amphitheater . . . for a gladiatorial show. But he neither rested its foundations on solid ground nor fastened the wooden supports securely . . . . The packed structure collapsed, falling both inwards and outwards . . . overwhelming a huge crowd of spectators and bystanders . . . . Fifty thousand people were mutilated or crushed in the disaster."

gladiator fights in Rome's main town square because of a remark by the first-century B.C. Roman architect Vitruvius. In his work titled *On Architecture,* he wrote: "The custom of giving gladiatorial shows in the forum has been handed down from our ancestors."

Over the years, the public fights became increasingly popular. So they drew more and more spectators, and it was necessary to provide seating for them. As in the case of circuses, such seating was at first made of wood. The seating was also temporary. Games officials put up the seats around a forum just prior to a public show and then dismantled them afterward. By the late second century B.C., freestanding, oval-shaped amphitheaters that could seat thousands of people were being constructed of wood. Some of these probably lasted a few years before they were dismantled. But many burned down and a few even collapsed, killing some of the spectators. It was clear that there was a pressing need for stronger, more permanent amphitheaters, ones made of stone.

It took tons of stone and countless laborers to create stone amphitheaters.

Chapter Two

First Stone Amphitheaters

The Romans knew that amphitheaters built of stone would be stronger and more permanent than those built of wood. However, they also realized that erecting a large stone structure took a long time and required the labor of many workers. Also, the heavy stone usually had to be hauled many miles to the work site. All of these factors made stone construction extremely expensive. So the transition from wooden arenas to stone ones happened very slowly.

The first all-stone amphitheater was completed in 80 B.C., about fifty years before Augustus established the Roman Empire. It was located in Pompeii, a seaside town about 140 miles (225 kilometers) southeast of Rome. The building's oval bowl has survived almost completely intact. It measured 445 by 341 feet (136 by 104 m) and held twenty thousand people, roughly the number of people who lived in the town. The

A Volcano Preserves the Past

Though Pompeii was a fairly average Roman town in most respects, it became unusually famous in modern times. A nearby volcano, Mount Vesuvius, erupted in A.D. 79 and buried the town in ash and other debris. The eruption erased Pompeii from the map. But the volcanic tomb also preserved much of the city, which was rediscovered in the 1700s. Many buildings, including the town's amphitheater, look essentially as they did almost twenty centuries ago.

arena floor, where the combats took place, was much lower than the level of the outside ground. So the thousands of tons of earth on the outside of the building enclosed and helped to support the heavy tiers of stone seats.

The Structure's Original Comforts

Standing inside the Pompeiian amphitheater can be an eerie experience. With Mount Vesuvius looming ominously in the distance, the amphitheater's stone walls and seats look practically the same as they did when they were first built. Some people feel almost as if they have been transported back into the past and that a group of gladiators might march out into the arena at any moment.

However, certain details needed to complete this illusion of the past coming to life are now missing. In particular, the amphitheater is rather bare compared to its original look. Back

This photograph shows the ruins of the amphitheater in Pompeii. Mount Vesuvius can be seen in the background.

in ancient times, spectators enjoyed numerous comforts and colorful features. The building was decorated with elegant tapestries and beautiful statues, for instance. And the people sat on soft cushions to make the stone seats more comfortable. They also snacked on fast food, including sausages, cheese, and cakes, sold at stands set up outside the structure or sold by roving vendors inside.

17

In addition, a large awning, or *velarium*, covered most of the seats. This was necessary because the heat from the Mediterranean sun can be very intense at midday. And if the spectators were not shaded from it, they would become severely sunburned. A team of specially trained slaves raised and lowered the awing by using ropes and pulleys.

Basic Features of Amphitheaters

The amphitheater at Pompeii proved very popular and often drew tourists from other parts of southern Italy. But it was very expensive to build and maintain. So for a long time no other Roman towns attempted to build their own all-stone arenas. Even Italy's largest city, Rome, lacked such a structure. In 29 B.C., about fifty years after the completion of Pompeii's amphitheater, a Roman general named Statilius Taurus built an arena in Rome. It was only partly made of stone, though. Much of it, perhaps including the seats, was constructed of wood. This made it **vulnerable** to serious damage by fire, and, in fact, a fire destroyed it about ninety years after it was built.

Though Taurus's amphitheater did not survive, historians believe that it probably looked much like the one at Pompeii. All Roman amphitheaters, then and later, had similar basic features. The arena floor, where the gladiators and animals fought, was oval-shaped and made of dirt. Around the floor stood a protective wall about 7 feet (2 m) or more tall. This was designed to separate the spectators from the action and keep them safe from wild animals.

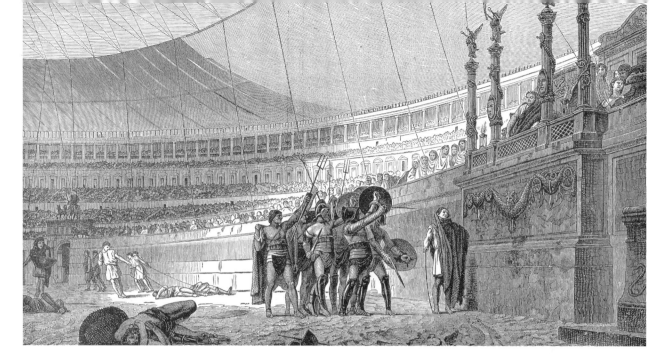

The seating section surrounding the arena floor was called the *cavea*. It was also in the shape of an oval and rose in tiers, just as in a modern sports stadium. The first tier of seats, located directly above the protective wall, was known as the **podium**. It was reserved seating for special people, such as high public officials and military generals. The next tier was where citizens of the wealthy, upper social classes sat. Members of the middle and lower classes, including slaves and foreigners, sat in the upper tiers.

Gladiators fought on the arena floor while important individuals, such as the emperor, sat on the podium.

Why the Colosseum Was Built

The fire that destroyed Taurus's amphitheater occurred in A.D. 64, fifty years after Augustus's death. By coincidence, this disaster proved to be the first link in the chain of events leading to the construction of the Roman capital's first and greatest all-stone amphitheater—the Colosseum. The so-called "great fire" raged for nine days and destroyed large portions of the city. When it was over, the emperor, Nero, organized ambitious rebuilding programs. Unfortunately, he was a very **conceited** person who cared mainly for himself and his personal pleasures. So much of the money and resources went into building his own private palace and park. The palace became known as the "Golden House."

Where Did Women Sit?

The first Roman emperor, Augustus, issued an **edict**—an official public statement having the force of law—about where women sat in amphitheaters. He ordered them to sit in the topmost tier, in the seats farthest away from the arena floor. His exact reasons for this edict are unknown. Perhaps he was trying to shelter women somewhat from the gruesome sight of blood-letting and death.

Nero—Tyrant and Murderer

Augustus's great-great grandson, Nero, reigned from A.D. 54 to 68. Unfortunately for Rome, Nero was far inferior to his famous ancestor, both as a ruler and as a person. A **tyrant** who persecuted the Christians and murdered his own mother and two wives, Nero angered many Romans. And when he took his own life rather than face justice, few, if any, mourned his passing.

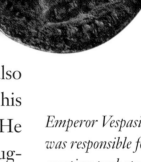

Over time, Nero proved to be not only conceited, but also a tyrant. This caused unrest and eventually rebellion, as his own generals and other high-placed people turned on him. He committed suicide. And after a brief but bloody power struggle, a general named Vespasian became emperor. An honest and productive ruler, Vespasian wanted to do whatever he could to erase Nero's memory. The new emperor also felt that it was high time for Rome to have a proper stone amphitheater. What better gesture could he make, he reasoned, than to tear down Nero's Golden House and erect the new arena in its place?

Thus, in the year A.D. 72, work began on the Colosseum. It would end up hosting thousands of public games over the centuries. Perhaps even more important, it would outlive the Empire itself and become one of the lasting symbols of Rome's greatness.

Emperor Vespasian was responsible for creating perhaps the best known amphitheater in the world.

21

The Colosseum stands as a monument to the creativity, strength, and determination of the ancient Romans.

Chapter Three

Building Amphitheaters

Erecting a stone amphitheater was an immense project requiring a great deal of time, money, talent, and just plain hard work. The most famous example, the Colosseum, is a case in point. Any visitor who stands outside or inside this structure can appreciate what an enormous task building it must have been, especially without the aid of modern machinery and steel girders. Its immense oval bowl measures 620 feet (189 m) by 513 feet (157 m) and it is 156 feet (48 m)

Workers hauled all the stones necessary to build the Colosseum while masons carved the stone in the appropriate shapes.

high. That is large enough to hold about 140 average-sized modern high school gyms!

It is no wonder, then, that the Colosseum took nine years to complete and cost the Roman government the equivalent of tens of millions of dollars in today's money. It also employed the Roman world's greatest **architects**, experts at designing buildings, as well as hundreds and at times thousands of workers. **Surveyors** were used to measure the site and make sure the building was level. Laborers quarried stone and transported it to the work site, and **masons** carved and built with stone. The project also required the labor of tool-makers, cart-makers, blacksmiths, carpenters, sculptors, painters, rope-makers, water-bearers, bakers and other food suppliers, and many others.

Laying the Foundation

The first major step in erecting a stone amphitheater like the Colosseum was to lay the foundation. The builders had to make sure that both the ground and the foundation were perfectly level. If they were not, the structure that rested on them would tilt slightly to one side or the other. And this would make the building unstable and prone to cracking or maybe even collapsing.

To ensure a level foundation, the surveyors used a device called a *chorobates*. It was about 20 feet (6 m) long and looked much like a wooden bench. About halfway down from the top, a crosspiece ran **horizontally**, or from side to side, from one leg to the other. Drawn on this crosspiece were two lines that were **vertical**, or up-and-down. And directly in front of the lines of the crosspiece hung small metal weights called **plumb bobs**. The strings holding the plumb bobs could always be counted on to be perfectly vertical. So by making the lines on the crosspiece match up with the strings of the plumb bobs, a surveyor could be sure that the *chorobates* was perfectly level. Then he peered through eyeholes cut into the wood and looked at the ground or foundation in the distance. If the level of the ground or foundation did not line up with the level of the crosspiece, he had his workers made the needed adjustments.

In addition to being perfectly level, an amphitheater's foundation had to be extremely strong. After all, when completed it would have to support millions of tons of stone, wood, dirt,

Concrete was used to make the amphitheater's foundation strong enough to support the weight of all of the spectators.

people, and animals. For the foundations of amphitheaters, as well as most other stone buildings, the Romans used a kind of concrete of their own invention. It was made from a mortar or cement called *pulvis Puteolanus*. This name came from the town of Puteoli, near Mount Vesuvius, the volcano that buried Pompeii. It was at Puteoli that the Romans collected a fine volcanic ash that constituted the main ingredient of their concrete. First they mixed the ash with water and a mineral called lime to produce the mortar. Then they created the finished concrete by adding coarse sand or gravel to the mortar. When the concrete dried, it became hard and durable and could support a great deal of weight.

Supports, Walls, and Ceilings

After the foundation of an amphitheater had been laid, the next step was to erect the building's **superstructure**, or skeleton. It was composed of the vertical and horizontal supports to which the walls and floors would later be attached. The vertical supports were called **piers**. Most of the piers used in the Colosseum were made of **travertine**, a durable and attractive kind of limestone.

From this cross section of the Colosseum, it is possible to see the design of the interior and exterior of the amphitheater.

At the same time that some gangs of workers were erecting piers and other supports, other gangs followed them putting up the walls. There were two general kinds of walls. And each was composed of two layers. One kind of wall had an inner core of Roman concrete, the same material used in the structure's foundation. The wall's **façade**, its front or outer layer, was made of baked bricks. The inside of the other kind of wall was made of *tufa*, a sort of stone that forms when volcanic ash is highly **compressed**, or squeezed under a great amount of weight. The outside was dressed with slabs of travertine.

Components of an Arch

A Roman arch is supported by two vertical piers, usually of stone. From the top of the piers, a series of wedge-shaped stones called **voussoirs** curve upward and inward and meet at a central stone at the top—the **keystone**. Roman arches were extremely strong.

This photograph shows an arch dating back to the early Roman Empire.

Other workers installed two of the major architectural features found throughout a Roman amphitheater. These were the **arch** and the **vault**. Both became **trademarks**, or identifying features, of Roman construction. An arch is a curved line at the top of a door, window, or other open space in a structure. Almost all of the doorways and other openings in the Colosseum were topped by arches. And there were 240 arches in the structure's outer wall alone. A vault is a curved or domed ceiling. Nearly all of the corridors leading to and around the Colosseum's seating section had vaulted ceilings.

29

Scaffolding and Lifting Devices

As construction progressed on an amphitheater, the outer walls grew taller and taller. To reach the higher levels, the workers stood on wooden **scaffolding** similar in some ways to the kind used in modern construction. The scaffolding needed to be supported so that it would not collapse and injure the workers. So they often attached the scaffolding to the wall on which they were working. The little holes into which they inserted the ends of the scaffolding are still visible on the outer surfaces of the Colosseum and other surviving Roman buildings.

Another challenge of working on the higher levels was lifting the heavy stones and other materials. To accomplish this task, the builders employed various cranes. One such crane consisted of a large circular cage with a treadmill inside. Several men climbed in and used muscle power to turn a pole running through the center of the device. There were ropes and pulleys attached to the pole and also to the weight they desired to lift. So as the pole turned, it pulled on the weight, raising it from the ground.

Archaeologists have found a sculpture carved in stone showing this very lifting device. They discovered it in a tomb belonging to a Roman family named the Haterii. It dates to about the time the Colosseum was built, so it seems certain that the builders of that structure utilized such a crane to raise stones to its upper levels. This was only one of several ways that Roman builders used ingenuity and sheer brute force to erect huge structures without the aid of modern machinery.

Scaffolding helped the Romans erect tall structures, such as amphitheaters or temples, as shown here.

This ancient Roman mosaic shows musicians performing in an amphitheater.

Chapter Four

Combat in a Roman Arena

Ancient Romans used their amphitheaters mainly to present public games and shows to masses of spectators. The opening ceremonies of such shows were festive and colorful. Typically, the fighters and other participants entered the arena in a parade known as the *pompa*. Acrobats, jugglers, and other circus-like performers accompanied them. All marched or danced around the arena to music produced by an orchestra consisting of flutes, trumpets, and drums. Sometimes a large

Background Music

Some evidence suggests that the musicians who played during the opening parade also played during the fighting. This would have created the same effect as the background music in a modern movie.

Women Gladiators

Not all gladiators were men. Occasionally the amphitheater games featured women gladiators. The emperor Domitian, who reigned from A.D. 81 to 96, liked watching women fight in the arena. He sometimes paired them against male dwarves, as well as against one another.

water-powered organ played too. The onlookers may have clapped their hands or stamped their feet in time to the music.

Eventually, the parade ended and the jugglers and other minor performers exited the arena. An official then inspected the fighters' weapons to make sure that they were well-sharpened. Finally, the fighters raised their weapons to the highest ranking official present, who was sometimes the emperor. "Those who are about to die salute you!" they recited in unison. And then the killing began.

The Way Society Viewed Gladiators

Some of the fighters who took part in ceremonies at the amphitheaters were gladiators, warriors trained to fight other warriors. They were mostly slaves, prisoners, and war captives who were forced to fight. But a few free individuals occasionally volunteered to become arena fighters. Some probably did so hoping to make some money, for there was a bonus paid for signing up and sometimes prize money for the winners. Whether they were slave or free, though, society looked down on all gladiators as crude and **unsavory** characters. Their low social status was summed up by the word *infamia*, meaning "bad reputation."

It perhaps seems odd that at the same time that Roman society scorned gladiators, the arena exploits of these fighters were greatly admired. Indeed, gladiators were often popular heroes with large fan followings like those of famous modern athletes. The reasons for this double standard regarding

Most gladiators were people who had no choice other than to battle each other.

gladiators are not completely clear. One Roman Christian writer, Tertullian, criticized it. "They love those they punish," he said. "They belittle those they esteem . . . . What kind of judgement is this?"

The Fighters and Their Battles

The gladiatorial fights that took place in amphitheaters were known as *munera*. This term meant "offerings to the dead." It derived from the fact that such fights originated as part of

This painting shows a retiarius *gladiator.*

funeral rites. The Romans borrowed the custom from another Italian people, the Etruscans. They believed that when a prominent man died, his spirit could not reach the afterlife without a blood sacrifice. So they staged fights to the death at funerals. Over time, the Romans transformed these private rituals into large-scale public shows.

Many different types of gladiators took part in the *munera*. One common type was called the **Samnite**. He was heavily armed, with a long sword or a lance, a metal helmet and other armor, and a large shield. The **Thracian** was another kind of gladiator. He carried a short, curved sword called a *sica* and a small round shield, the *parma*. Still another kind of fighter was known as a *retiarius*, or "net-thrower." As his name suggests, he wielded a large net, with which he tried to trip or entangle his opponent. He also defended himself with a long **trident**, or three-pronged spear. There were also gladiators who specialized in fighting with two swords at a time. Others used **lassos** (looped ropes) or rode on horses and chariots. Some even fought blindfolded by helmets with no eyeholes.

When two of these professional fighters met each other in the center of an amphitheater, the encounter could end in several different ways. One common outcome, of course, was

Thumbs Up, Down, or Inward?

The spectators in an amphitheater may have used the familiar "thumbs-up" to spare a fighter and "thumbs-down" to call for his death. However, some scholars disagree. They suggest that people spared a gladiator with a thumbs-down, a signal for the winner to drop his sword. And they called for death by pointing their thumbs toward their chests, indicating a sword through the heart.

when one gladiator killed the other. As the crowd cheered the winner, some young boys ran out and cleaned the bloodstains from the sand. At the same time, some men dragged away the dead body to clear the area for the next match.

Another common outcome was when one gladiator fell to the ground wounded. He raised up one finger, a signal that meant he wanted the emperor or other high official to spare his life. Usually, the official first consulted the spectators. They shouted and used hand signals to indicate either "life" or

In some fights, the crowd could determine whether the losing gladiator lived or died.

"death." Still another way a match might end was in a draw. If the emperor or games official felt that both fighters were evenly matched and had fought bravely, he allowed both to leave the arena.

The Wild Beast Shows

Besides the gladiator, the other kind of fighter featured in a Roman amphitheater was the *venator*, or "hunter." He or she took part in a wild beast show called a *venatio*, meaning

This fresco painting found on the wall of an amphitheater in Merida shows a venator fighting a wild beast.

"hunt." Both of these terms are a bit misleading because no one actually hunted down the animals as hunters do in the wild. Instead, the *venatores* fought with and killed the animals. Or the animals were prodded to fight with one another. In the third kind of *venatio*, condemned prisoners were attacked and eaten by half-starved beasts. And in the fourth and much tamer variety, trained animals, like those in modern circuses, performed.

The animals were captured, often at great expense, from all parts of the Empire and beyond. There were elephants from India and Africa, bears from central Europe, lions and leopards from Africa, and the **Near East**, tigers from Persia and India, horses from Spain, and crocodiles from Egypt, to name only a few. The numbers of animals slaughtered in these shows was sometimes enormous. For instance, about nine thousand of them died in the Colosseum in the three months following the amphitheater's opening in A.D. 80.

More fortunate were those animals that were trained to perform tricks. Monkeys were very popular. Sometimes they wore soldiers' uniforms and drove miniature chariots drawn by goats. Trained lions held rabbits and cats in their jaws without harming them. And elephants danced, walked tightropes, and ate food from plates like people do. For those few Romans who did not care for the more brutal spectacles of humans and animals killing one another, these trained animals were a welcome relief.

Against the Slaughter

Most Romans enjoyed the brutality of the arena. But at least a few found it distasteful and pointless. The famous senator and public speaker Cicero, for example, asked: "What pleasure can a civilized man find when either a helpless human being is mangled by a very strong animal, or a magnificent animal is stabbed again and again by a hunting spear?"

Visitors to the Colosseum can only imagine the splendor of this amazing structure in ancient times.

Chapter Five

The Fate of Amphitheaters

Entering the Colosseum today, visitors are greeted by a sight very different than the one the ancient Romans beheld. Gone are all the statues and other decorations, along with the great awning that once shaded the spectators. The original stone seats are missing, too. And many of the arches, vaults, and corridors that honeycombed the rising tiers of the seating section are also missing or crumbling. Overall, the building is a mere skeleton of what it was in its original glory.

This photograph shows the ruins of an amphitheater in Pozzuo.

A few of the other Roman amphitheaters, including the one at Pompeii, are better preserved than the Colosseum. On the other hand, others are in poorer shape. All of these ruins are now viewed as priceless treasures, part of the surviving heritage of a vanished culture. So they are carefully protected and maintained. The fascinating story of how these once great monuments fell into decay and were later rediscovered and rescued begins in the final years of the Roman Empire.

The End of the Roman Games

Year after year, century after century, the Colosseum and other Roman amphitheaters witnessed the thrill and horror of people and animals fighting and dying. But late in the fourth century, the nature of these shows changed. The main reason was the rapid rise of Christianity in that same century. Christian leaders had long condemned the amphitheater games, calling the gladiatorial combats murder. Eventually, the emperors and their advisors were all Christians. And they closed the gladiator schools and banned arena combats

Vandals, one of the many different groups of "barbarians," who attacked the city of Rome.

43

between human fighters. The amphitheaters remained open and still drew large crowds. But the main attractions were now wild beast shows and wrestling matches.

In time, though, even these amphitheater shows ended. This was because the Roman realm itself declined and eventually ceased to exist. In the fourth and fifth centuries, large groups of people from northern Europe and western Asia poured into the Roman provinces. They did not have cities and most could not read or write. So the Romans called them "barbarians." In A.D. 476, a barbarian leader forced the Roman emperor, Romulus Augustulus, from the throne. No emperor took his place.

Centuries of Decay

In the two centuries following the fall of the Roman government, the populations of Rome and many other cities significantly decreased. The majority of those who remained were poor. And they could no longer afford to stage large-scale public games and shows. Neither could they afford to repair and maintain most of the large buildings, including the

amphitheaters. So these structures slowly began to crumble and fall into ruin. Grass began to grow in the now silent bleachers of the Colosseum and other Roman arenas.

As the centuries wore on, the old amphitheaters continued to decay. Bushes and trees grew up inside them, and earthquakes and other natural disasters damaged them. In the year 847 a large earthquake rocked the Colosseum. And in 1231, an even larger quake caused the entire southwestern part of the building's outer wall to collapse.

Meanwhile, the local inhabitants took most of the travertine, marble, and other fine building stones. They used these to make houses and other smaller, less impressive structures. No one cared about the looting of the old ruins, for the people

This painting shows an amphitheater falling into ruin after the end of the Roman Empire.

had forgotten their past and the greatness of their ancestors. In fact, eventually no one even remembered the original purpose of the amphitheaters. For example, a twelfth-century guidebook to Rome mistakenly claimed that the Colosseum had been a religious temple.

Efforts to Preserve the Past

The Colosseum in the Moonlight

After visiting the Colosseum in 1832, American landscape painter Thomas Cole wrote: "It is stupendous, yet beautiful in its destruction. . . . He who would see and feel the grandeur of the Colosseum must spend his hour there, at night, when the moon is shedding over it its magic splendor."

However, in early modern times, beginning in the 1700s, the sad fate of Rome's amphitheaters and other ancient buildings began to change for the better. This was because European scholars rediscovered the glories of the ancient civilizations of Greece and Rome. Popular writers and artists traveled to Rome. They described the Colosseum and other old structures in romantic terms, calling them precious relics of the past.

At the same time, archaeologists began to excavate and examine these ancient structures. The result was an increasing effort to protect and preserve them. In 1825, for example, excavators installed large stone supports in sections of the Colosseum. These saved the remains of the outer wall from further collapse. And in 1870, workmen cleared away the trees, bushes, and other undergrowth that had choked the building's interior. In 1992, a huge new restoration effort began on the Colosseum. The goal of the project was to repair and clean all damaged sections.

Today, as such efforts continue, the Colosseum and other ancient amphitheaters remain popular tourist attractions.

Thousands of people from around the world come each year, some to marvel at the skill of the builders. Others are fascinated and often moved by the knowledge that so many millions of people and animals met bloody ends in these

Work was done to restore the façade of the Colosseum in 1996.

structures. Indeed, when standing inside them one can almost see the violent combats and hear the screams of the crowds. And in this way a long vanished civilization comes to life in the mind's eye. As the famous English novelist Charles Dickens put it when he visited the Colosseum in 1846: "To climb its upper halls, and look down on ruin. . . all about it. . . is to see the ghost of old Rome, [a] wicked wonderful old city, haunting the very ground on which its people trod."

Timeline

B.C.

753	This year is the traditional founding date for the city of Rome.
509	The Roman Republic, a representative type of government largely controlled by a legislature, the Senate, is established.
146	The Romans complete their conquest of Greece. They now control almost all the lands bordering the Mediterranean Sea.
80	The residents of Pompeii, in southwestern Italy, erect the first all-stone amphitheater.
63	Birth of Octavian, who will later become Augustus, the first Roman emperor.
29	A Roman military general named Statilius Taurus builds an amphitheater partially made of stone in the city of Rome.
27	The Senate bestows on Octavian the name of Augustus. Historians usually mark this as the beginning of the Roman Empire.

A.D.

27	In the Italian town of Fidenae, a wooden amphitheater collapses, injuring or killing as many as 50,000 people.
57	The Roman emperor Nero builds a large wooden amphitheater in Rome.
64	A devastating fire destroys about two-thirds of Rome. Nero begins building a palace, the Golden House, on some of the land cleared after the blaze.

68	Nero commits suicide and a short but bloody power struggle begins.
69	A general named Vespasian wins the struggle and becomes emperor.
72	Under Vespasian's architects, work begins on the Colosseum.
79	Vespasian dies and is succeeded by his eldest son, Titus. Also, the volcano Mount Vesuvius erupts, burying the town of Pompeii, along with its famous amphitheater.
80	Titus inaugurates the Colosseum by staging large-scale gladiatorial and wild beast shows.
107	A popular emperor named Trajan sponsors games lasting 123 days in the Colosseum.
ca. 430	The last gladiatorial fights take place in the Colosseum.
476	Romulus Augustulus, the last Roman emperor, is forced to vacate his throne.
1231	A large earthquake causes part of the Colosseum's outer wall to collapse.
ca. 1500	Pope Alexander VI allows builders to use the Colosseum as a commercial quarry. Thousands of tons of the amphitheater's stones are removed for use in newer structures.
1744	Pope Benedict XIV issues an edict protecting the Colosseum from further destruction.
1870	Italian workman clear the tangles of trees and undergrowth that have grown up inside the Colosseum.
1992	The Italian government begins a major restoration of the Colosseum.

Glossary

amphitheater—a wooden or stone building used by the ancient Romans to stage gladiatorial fights and wild animals shows. The Latin term was *amphitheatrum*, meaning "double theater."

aqueduct—an artificial channel designed to carry water from one place to another

arch—a curved line of stone or other material at the top of a door, window, bridge support, or other open space in a structure

architect—an expert at designing buildings

arena—the central section of an ancient Roman amphitheater, where the fighting took place. The term *arena* is also sometimes used to describe the entire building.

auger—a drill, usually metal-tipped, that one turns by hand

cavea—the seating section in an ancient Roman theater or amphitheater

chorobates—a device used by ancient Roman surveyors to make sure that the ground or a building's foundation was level

circus—a long building used by the ancient Romans for chariot racing

compressed—squeezed under a great amount of weight

conceited—very impressed with oneself

edict—an official public statement having the force of law

façade—the front or outer layer of a building or other object

forum—a public square

gladiator—in ancient Rome, a person trained to fight, usually to the death, in the public games

hemisphere—the area enclosed in a half-circle, like half of a pie

horizontal—from side to side or from left to right

infamia—a Latin word meaning "bad reputation." It was often applied to gladiators, actors, and other people seen as social outcasts.

keystone—the central, topmost stone in an arch

lasso—a rope tied into a loop and thrown in an effort to entangle and capture an animal or person

legion—in the ancient Roman army, a group of about five thousand soldiers who traveled, camped, and fought together

mason—an expert in carving and building with stone

munera—a Latin word meaning "offerings to the dead," it was the general term applied to gladiatorial shows

Near East—sometimes called the Middle East, it is the region that includes the modern countries of Iraq, Iran, Jordan, Israel, and Egypt

parma—a small round shield carried by the gladiator type known as the Thracian

pier—a vertical support in a building

plumb bob—a small weight attached to a string that surveyors and others use to determine whether something is vertical

podium—in a Roman amphitheater, the lowest seating section, located directly above the arena. It was customarily reserved for royalty or high-ranking officials.

point—a tool used by ancient masons to chip, carve, or make indentations in stone. Also called a punch.

pompa—the parade-like ceremony that opened various Roman games

pulvis Puteolanus—the mortar the Romans used to make concrete. It was named after the town of Puteoli, near the volcano Mount Vesuvius, where they gathered the volcanic ash used to make the mortar.

retiarius—a kind of gladiator who wielded a net and a trident

Samnite—a type of gladiator who wore armor, a heavy metal helmet, and wielded a long sword or a lance

scaffolding—a wooden framework erected beside an unfinished building for the workers to stand on

sica—a short, curved sword used by a Thracian gladiator

superstructure—in construction work, a skeleton, composed of vertical and horizontal supports to which the walls and floors are attached

surveyor—an expert at measuring the land, especially areas where buildings, roads, and other structures are planned

thatch—bundled plant stems and branches, sometimes used for the walls or roofs of primitive or simple structures

Thracian—a kind of gladiator who defended himself with a short sword (the *sica*) and a round shield (the *parma*). He was so named because these were the weapons used by warriors in Thrace, a region in extreme northern Greece.

trademark—a recognizable identifying feature or characteristic of a people, country, organization, or other entity

travertine—a durable, creamy-white kind of limestone commonly employed in ancient Roman construction

trident—a long, three-pronged spear

tufa—a lightweight variety of stone formed when volcanic ash is highly compressed

tyrant—an overbearing or cruel ruler

unsavory—disgusting or repulsive

vault—a curved or domed ceiling

velarium—an awning that the ancient Romans spread across

the top of their theaters and amphitheaters to protect the spectators from the sun

venatio—a Latin word translated as "hunts." It was used as a general term to describe any of the wild animal shows staged in amphitheaters.

venator—a "hunter" in the wild animal shows that were staged in amphitheaters

vertical—running up and down or from top to bottom

voussoir—a wedge-shaped stone, one of several used to make the curved portion of an arch

vulnerable—open to possible damage or attack

To Find Out More

Books

Corbishley, Mike. *The World of Architectural Wonders*. New York: Peter Bedrick Books, 1996.

Greene, Jacqueline Dembar. *Slavery in Ancient Greece and Rome*. Danbury, CT: Franklin Watts, 2000.

Jessup, Joanne. *The X-Ray Picture Book of Big Buildings of the Ancient World*. Danbury, CT: Franklin Watts, 1993.

Nardo, Don. *Games of Ancient Rome*. San Diego: Lucent Books, 2000.

———. *Greek and Roman Sport*. San Diego: Lucent Books, 1999.

———. *The Roman Colosseum*. San Diego: Lucent Books, 1998.

———. *Roman Roads and Aqueducts*. San Diego: Lucent Books, 2001.

Peach, Susan, and Anne Millard. *The Romans*. London: Usborne, 1990.

Simpson, Judith. *Ancient Rome*. New York: Time-Life Books, 1997.

Organizations and Online Sites

Illustrated History of the Roman Empire
http://www.roman-empire.net/children/index.html
This site contains a wealth of information on life during the Roman Empire.

Kid Info
http://www.kidinfo.com/World_History/AncientRome.html
This online site is a great starting point for young readers who want to learn more about ancient Rome. It provides many links to topics about ancient Rome, including architecture and important buildings, such as the Colosseum.

Odyssey Online

http://www.emory.edu/CARLOS/ODYSSEY/

This site contains a wealth of information on ancient Rome as well as other ancient cultures.

Roman Colosseum

http://www.greatbuildings.com/buildings/Roman_Colosseum.html

This online site is an excellent general resource about the Colosseum, with links to related sites. It also provides a list of interesting books about this famous structure.

The Romans

http://www.bbc.co.uk/education/romans/home.html

Learn about the Roman army, Roman roads and places, and other aspects of life in ancient Rome from this interesting online site.

Vitruvius, Ancient Architect

http://www.cs.cmu.edu/People/Vit/vitruvius.html

This online site contains a brief biography of the first-century Roman architect, Vitruvius. He wrote an architectural manual that was used by later Roman architects who worked on many amphitheaters.

A Note on Sources

Writing any book about Rome or other ancient societies requires finding and reading many sources, both ancient and modern. Often such sources take the form of books. Articles written for monthly or quarterly journals and magazines are also important sources used by historians. The number of required sources for a volume like this one is especially large. This is because the book touches on numerous different subjects, including Roman architecture and building methods, Roman games, and several other aspects of Roman civilization. Literally hundreds of recently written sources are available on these subjects. And more are published all the time.

Merely locating so many sources is potentially very time-consuming for a writer. In writing this book, however, I was able to save a good deal of time. Because writing about ancient Greece and Rome is my specialty, I own a large number of books about Rome, which I consult frequently. Some were written mainly for scholars to read, so they are very detailed and technical. Others are more general and easy to read. Of the more general sources on Roman architecture, Peter Quennell's book about the Colosseum is one of the best and most readable. L. Sprague de Camp's *The Ancient Engineers*, though slightly more advanced, is fascinating, valuable, and well worth the effort. About gladiators and their colorful but brutal combat, Michael Grant's volume on that topic is an excellent general source. And Adkins' and Adkins' *Handbook to Life in Ancient Rome* is among the better volumes about ancient Roman life written recently for general readers.

—*Don Nardo*

Index

Numbers in *italics* indicate illustrations.

About the Author

Don Nardo is a historian and award-winning writer who has published numerous books about the ancient world. Among these are *The Age of Pericles*, about the golden age of ancient Greece; *The Battle of Marathon*, which tells the exciting story of how the soldiers of ancient Athens defeated a much larger force of invading Persians; *Life of a Roman Soldier*, a fascinating study of the ancient Roman military; *Empires of Mesopotamia*, an overview of the ancient Sumerians, Babylonians, and Assyrians; and biographies of the great Roman general, Julius Caesar, and the wily Egyptian queen, Cleopatra. Mr. Nardo lives with his wife Christine in Massachusetts.